Conte
Introc

The Geordie Character
Conversation (Chat or Taakin')
Eating and eating out (Eatin' and Eatin'oot)
Drinking (BooZin' or On the Hoy)
Toon Weekend (the pub and the match)
- Oot on the Toon
- On the Tap or on the Pull
- The Toon - Newcastle United and the match

Entertaining at home - When Geordie has guests
Shopping (Therapy)
Essential Words and Phrases

Features

Advanced Geordie!!
Musical terms
Geordie haka
Gentleman v Geordie Ettyket
Courtesy of Brendan Healy
Great North Run Ettyket
Geordies at the seaside
Geordie Jeff Stelling
Geordie-ness Test

Introduction

Let's start with a Disclaimer! – The text in this book is meant to be a **little** tongue in cheek and a bit of fun and no offence is meant or implied to anyone, Geordie or non-Geordie.
Only try to speak Geordie if you are one, if you have been coached by one or you take great care with the advice in this book.
Visitors to the Toon are allowed to engage with Geordies so they can improve their pronunciation.
He or she is mentioned in this book. It is mainly from my perspective as a man. But all of it applies to Geordie lasses very much as it does to the Geordie lads. Geordie Lasses are amongst the most fun in the world!

Controversially, this book **may** even apply to Makems (see definition later) as well as Geordies!!!!

This book is for two distinct groups of people. First of all, it is for Geordies to remind them of their heritage and the way they are. They are unique and special and are proud of who they are and their way of life. Non – Geordies must respect Propa and Posh Geordies alike. More of that later!
The second group of people are those who visit Geordieland and want to be like Geordies for a short period of time and experience what it is like to be one of the best groups of people in the world!!!
For the sake of clarity, and possible controversy, and for the purposes of this book, Geordieland is defined as anywhere in Northumberland and 5 miles north or south of the River Tyne. That definition will upset some people but, howay, it's my book!!!!

This book is sometimes serious, sometimes not so serious - if you think it is humorous, great! If anyone is offended - sorry and tough at the same time!

To sum up the intro

When in Geordie land, do as the Geordies do.

The Geordie Character

The origin of the word Geordie is not clear cut. Some people think it referred to the people of Newcastle because they supported George I and George II in the Jacobite Risings of 1715 and 1745. It was a term to distinguish the city's residents from others in the region, who backed the Stuarts.

Other main contenders come from mining. For a north-east colliery worker as George was a common pitman's name or a nickname for George Stephenson's safety-lamp which was used by the miners themselves.
However, one thing in my mind is certain, the Geordie character is born out of our history of mining, shipbuilding, railways and football. Some might add their drinking habits are quite famous. I leave that to your opinion once you have read this book and been out on the Toon for a night (or two)!

The families of coal miners and shipyard workers experienced harsh social justice and their experience has honed their character and they hold great pride in their achievements. Greatest among them is that the area can lay a very strong claim to be the origin of the industrial revolution.

Geordie communities are close. We are a friendly lot. We welcome strangers, we talk to anyone. Geordies have a warmth which welcomes everyone. We are caring and most are always kind. We are sensitive and don't mind showing our emotions – note Paul Gascoigne. Posh and Propa Geordies alike do not mind 'a little watta comin' doon thor cheeks'.

But if you're a Geordie, what do you have to cry about, anyway?

'He's a reet bubbla' him.

We rarely show weakness, we never say things like 'I divvent feel well' or 'the dogs ill' or 'the wife has left us'!

A Geordie will help anyone. We can forgive but not forget.
If you cross a Geordie, don't expect support in the future. A Geordie is a giver and objects to takers. We see ourselves as the underdog, ask any Newcastle United fan why!!!!

Geordies are very playful and mischievous, that's why they wind people up or take the mickey (piss). At every opportunity Geordies take the mickey about anything. He or she pushes their luck – naughty Geordies look to be a little playful. So, don't take offence if you think a Geordie is being insulting. It's their way of being friendly!

Geordies never whinge. Why would they? They are cool, hard(phyisically) and have an accent to die for!!!
However, a word of caution. The Geordie dialect is learned over decades and don't try it if you can't do it, it doesn't sound right! However, help is at hand because later in this book there are tips of how to pronounce words and a number of phrases which will make you feel at home here in Geordieland.

Geordieland was built in coal mines and shipyards. Geordies are fiercely proud of their heritage, passionate about everything they do and they do it to the fullest of their ability, none so much as drinking (see later)! Geordies invented and developed the railways, they built great factories, they built great ships, they provided the country with the fuel to make this country great.

We love local heroes and we have had a few over the years!
Some of the greatest men and women in history were born and bred in Geordieland - Earl Grey, George Stephenson, Robert Stephenson, William Armstrong, Sir Bobby Robson, Grace Darling, the Venerable Bede, Emily Wilding Davison, St Oswald, Catherine Cookson, St Cuthbert, Admiral Cuthbert Collingwood, Joseph Swan and Dame Flora Robson, etc. etc.

There are many Geordies in our society today who make it great – Alun Armstrong, Sting, Steve Cram, Brendan Foster, Mark Knopfler, Paul Gascoigne, Rowan Atkinson, Tim Healy, Neal Tennant, Ian La Frenais, Wendy Craig, Lauren Laverne, Hank Marvin, Anne Reid, Cheryl, Ant and Dec, Bryan Ferry, Chris Ramsey, Sara Davies, Brain Johnson, Ann Cleeves, Lee Hall, Eric Idle, Alexander Armstrong, Ridley Scott, Sarah Millican and Ross Noble to name but a few.

Even the Scots recognise the Geordie as an Honorary Scot. Not so sure we recognize them as Honorary Geordies!!!!! The Irish visit us in their droves because we are alike.

However, in some eyes, Geordieland is the end of civilization and I would argue we have some of the greatest historical and cultural assets in the country – Hadrian's Wall, the Town Walls, The Central Station, Grey Street, The Angel, the Tyne Bridge, the Great North Run, Greggs, The Sage Gateshead, The Hancock Museum, The Discovery Museum, China Town and loads of Castles in Northumberland. We even let Kittiwakes have home on the Tyne Bridge!

When a Geordie goes travelling and he returns he knows he is coming home when he sees those things that are important to him – the Angel, the Tyne, the Tyne Bridge, the Central Station, Greys monument.

If you have any of these quirks you could have Geordie genes!!!
Finally, there are two types of Geordie, Posh and Propa. A Posh Geordie has a very mild Geordie accent with a hint of proper English. They sound like a Geordie but they try to pronounce certain words in the Queens English. It doesn't sound quite right. It sounds a bit like someone who speaks the Queens English trying to speak Geordie. It just sounds wrong!!! They also have a hint of poshness. A Propa Geordie speaks **flewent** Geordie!

Geordie Jeff Stelling

There is a reason why people in Newcastle are so happy: these are the smiles of people who know they won the lottery of life and have been born a Geordie. Jeff Stelling knows this: he launched into an impassioned defence of our fair city after a set of disparaging comments were made on TalkSport.
Said Jeff of a caller dissing the Toon:
"He has probably never been to St James Park.
"He has probably never had a night out in the Bigg Market.
"He has probably never eaten at any of the wonderful restaurants.
"He has never appreciated the marvellous architecture of Grey Street.
"He'll never have been to the Theatre Royal.
"Never have been to the Racecourse.
"He'll never have strode along the Quayside in the shadow of the Tyne Bridge.
"He's never had a Newky Brown. (Jeff, the word Newky is so wrong!)

Conversation – 'Chat' or 'Taakin' in Geordieland

On arriving in the Toon when you meet someone, greet them with *'Y'aall reet'*. This means 'Are you well'
Some use the term *'What fettle'*
Some say *'Noo then'*
Your response should be *'Whey aye, Champion!'*

When you want to leave someone, you must say *'Aam gannin' yem'*, this means 'I am going home'.

When agreeing with someone, you must say *'Whey aye man'*

When disagreeing with someone, a Posh Geordie might say *'Hadaway and loss yersel'*. A Propa Geordie will say *'Hadaway and shite man'*

Manners are important to Geordies.
Posh Geordies say *'Thank You'*.
Propa Geordies say *'Cheers'* or *'Ta'*,

If you don't understand or didn't hear a question, don't answer at all or answer with a grunt.

Howay is a common word used by Geordies. It is mostly used when encouraging someone or a team. Shout *'Howay'* for example, when at a football match.
However, 'Howay' can have several meanings - get a grip, come on, or 'what the hell are yer deein' (What are you doing?)
When someone is expressing displeasure at your actions i.e. if a Geordie is bumped and spills his beer, he will shout *'Howay man!'* with great indignity.

One of the main communication rules for Geordies is to shout when having a conversation. Posh Geordies are slightly refined and only raise their voices when with their mates. Propa Geordies shout at the top of their voices when with their mates especially after a few drinks. (This optional for non-Geordies)

When someone upsets a Geordie so much you may think he may want to fight, 'Howay an' Aa'll smash yer face in'. Normally they don't mean it. It is a bit of bravado, what they really mean is take that back or I'll kiss you! All geordies are non-violent!

At every opportunity Geordie lasses compliment their mates about their hair, clothes, shoes, makeup etc etc etc. Whenever you want to say that something is good you could say -
'It's canny like' – which really is an understatement of how good something is.
Or *'It's a Belter'* or *'It's a Propa belter'*

Whatever happens, Propa Geordies (especially geordie lasses) never admit to being wrong. And it's never their fault, *like.*

Geordies use the word *'Like'* **A LOT**, in fact you can use it after every sentence if you want. No one will notice.
They also use the word *'Man'* **A LOT**. It means something different in different contexts. For example, *'Howay Man'* indicates a little bit of frustration. This is commonly expressed at the match when the Toon aren't playing very well.
Or
"Howay man, had ya watta, divvin' be a workyticket". This means 'Hold on my friend, do not upset me'

A third phrase used often is *'Y'knaa'* which means 'you know'. Again, you could end every sentence with *'Y'knaa'*

Posh Geordies can have a conversation about anything. Propa Geordies can also have a conversation about anything but nobody else understands a word they say. They are excellent spy material!!

Many more words and phrases are laid out later in the book for those who would like to learn more of the Geordie language.

Frankly my dear man neither do I!

Wor lass dissent understand me y'knaa

Courtesy of Brendan Healy

Three situations when you **don't** want to hear a Geordie voice.

- 'Norse, Scalpel'. (Nurse, Scalpel)

- 'Good evening, Ladies and Gentlemen, This evenin' w' will be flyin' at thorty six thooosand feet!' (Good Evening Ladies and Gentlemen, This evening we will be flying at 30,000 feet'

- 'Howay yer hona, me client didn't dee it'. (My client is innocent, My Lord!)

Eatin' and eatin' oot

Food is referred to as *'Bait'* or *'Scran'* For example -
'Eat yer Bait'
'Doon yer Scran'

When eating cake, Posh Geordies use a fork, Propa Geordies get stuck in and grab a piece and do not pick their nose at the same time.

Try any food that is given to you. Always say the food is good, unless, of course, it is shite! Propa geordies eat everything on a plate and mop up the dregs with bread. Never leave food on the plate – Geordies never waste food or **drink – especially drink!**

Both Posh and Propa Geordies put their elbows on the table when eating. It helps to keep them from falling over after a few beers. It is also a friendly gesture to show they are interested in the chat.

It is acceptable to make noise while eating.
Geordies can speak with their mouth full, food shouldn't get in the way of chatting with your mates or getting your point across or making a quip or a joke. Chat at the table can get a bit messy!

How to eat a pie

Take the pie out of its container and hold it in both sets of fingers and bite the end off the pie and suck the contents a bit at a time out from the top squeezing gently at the same time eating some of the pastry.
PC in Geordie doesn't mean Politically Correct it means Pie Consumption or Pie Content.

Geordie delicacies include stotties (Flattish bread), singing hinnies, Pan haggerty, tripe (essential after the Blaydon Race), black pudding, ham and pease pudding, sausage rolls, pies and anything from Greggs.
A steak bake from Greggs replenishes salt after a heavy session on the drink or returning from holiday at Newcastle airport!
Feeding children a Greggs pasty is a generally a Geordie pacifier or in some cases it is referred to as a Geordie dummy.

When buying sweets (bullets) or unhealthy food, refer to it as **ket**.

When buying cake pronounce it as **'kyek' (or Caake))**

When trying to cool down hot food or drink you **'blaa it'** cool.

It is not regarded as good manners to **bowk** (belch or vomit) in public but a few Geordies do.

Drinkin' ('Boozin' or 'on the Hoy')

On Fridays, Geordies are often heard saying *'Aam ganna get mortal the neet', 'Aam ganna get blathered (or bladdered) the neet'* or *'Aam ganna get palatik the neet'.*
This means they are going to drink as much as they can without spilling a drink and then they will fall down and get their mates to carry them home!

Posh and Propa Geordies always get their round in - skipping a round is a Southerner's trick. Always pay your round and keep an eye out for those who don't !
One of my favourite sayings when drinking in a round is :
'It's like a desert in here' - a cry from someone in a round who has finished his drink.

When drinking, Geordies will often say *'Get that doon yer neck'* This means drink that as fast as you can, there's another one on the way.

Geordie men drink beer *(pronounced 'beor')*. Drinking propa beer is for Propa Geordies, Lager or plastic beer is for wimps. Can any Geordie claim to be a Propa Geordie if they drink Lager – Howay! (get a grip!) Sorry, this is a personal view!!!

The beer of choice for older Geordies is the plastic beer, John Smiths.
Propa Geordies drink Newcastle Brown Ale, but young Geordies can't take it.
Many enlightened Geordies drink real ale which is propa beer!
Newcastle Brown Ale is traditionally the drink of the Geordies. It is referred to as dog or derg - **never** 'newky brown'. Only drink it in a schooner. Don't drink too many of the dog, it is stronger than you think, it might come back and bite yer!

Tek nee notice!
He aalways dis this
when it's his torn
for the beors

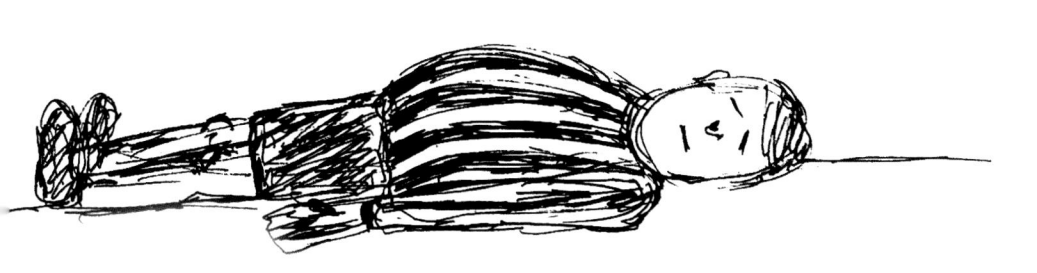

If someone offers you beer, drink it. If they offer you wine – say 'Sorry I don't drink fruit juice!'
Do not mix wine with beer, it makes the drink go cloudy or a funny colour. When it comes to drinking Geordies are vegetarians, they drink beer. The argument goes – beer is made from hops, hops are plants, therefore beer is a salad!

Aa divvent drink fruit juice!

No beer left- Do you want a glass of wine?

Drinking spirit chasers or shots is for young unenlightened Geordies who generally have a lot to learn. How can yer have a propa session if yer drink shots and have t' be taken yem after an hour! Again, another personal point of view!

Geordie women drink anything! However, they often drink Prosecco and some have even tried a half of lager. But many can drink Geordie Lads under the table.

Geordies will drink with anyone. Many think they can drink their drinking partner under the table. Be very wary of taking on any Geordie, male or female, in a drinking competition, you are likely to lose, unless you have Geordie Genes and you are not aware of!

Never leave part of a pint, always finish your drink. It is very bad form to leave any alcohol in a glass.

If a pint of beer has a large head, a Geordie would ask the bar tender 'Can you put a whisky in that?' - if the answer is 'Yes' the reply is 'Well fill it up then!'

If one of your mates is expected to join a session and he or she is late. Buy them a pint and when they arrive tell them 'There's one in the pump'

Never buy your mates a half pint, or say 'Aa'll hev a half this time'.
It is unheard of in Geordieland.

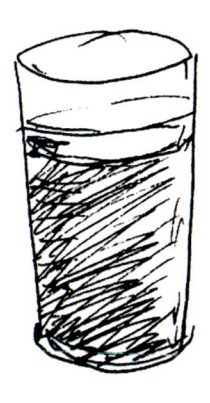

Can you put a whisky in there barman?...

Yes of course

Well fill it up then !!!

If you must drink soft drinks, drink Fentimans, the soft drink of choice for both Posh and Propa Geordies.

When you drink as much 'beor' as Geordies do you have to go to the toilet (loo or bathroom for non geordies).

Geordies have various descriptions about going to the toilet -
'Aa'm ganna spray the Daisies'
'Aa'm ganna point Percy at the porcelain'
'Aa'm ganna spend-a penny'
'Aa'm gannin for a pittle'
'Aa'm gannin t' the little boys room'
'Aa'm gannin t' the bog'
Or best *'A'am gannin t' the netty!'*

The Toon weekend – the pub and the match

Now that you understand the etiquette of drinking in Geordieland, you need to understand when most of the drink gets drunk !
But before that, it is essential to get the dress code right for a session on the drink !

Men

Never wear a coat or a jacket in the Toon. Never wear a jumper in public in the toon.
Propa Geordies are hard and can stand freezing cold temperatures (Scott of the Antarctic would have been the first man to get to the South Pole if he had a Geordie with him!). Geordies have vowed not to wear such appareil until the Toon win the Premier league (that's when hell freezes over!).

Women

The above applies to Geordie lasses but they must insist on showing as much flesh as possible that modesty will allow. It's great being a Geordie lad watching aal the lasses in the toon!! Always wear high heels that make you look like you're walking on moving cobblestones in a hurricane !

Oot on the Toon - Pub crawls

All Geordies know every pub, club and watering hole in the toon. A propa Geordie doesn't plan a pub crawl because it's in their blood. It's instinctive, intuitive and could do it with one with their eyes closed and throats open.
Always walk 4 abreast on the pavement.
Everyone defers to the doorman at the club.
Lads cower to the doorman at the nightclub queue.
Geordie lasses must flirt with the doorman at the nightclub.
Geordie lasses always dance with their handbag on the floor next to them.
Never get on the tables to dance until you have a least 3 drinks.
Lasses never go to the netty alone, they prefer to go with their best mate.
Lads go whenever they need to, which is quite often!

News
When Hell Freezes Over!

Is the toon ganna win something this year?

On the Tap or on the Pull (Meeting Young Ladies)

If a Geordie lad is knocked back by a girl, they always say thank you.
but then tell their mates she must be a lesbian.
When trying to compliment a young lady tell her she is a **'reet Bonny lass'**
Do not refer to the lady as a **bord** (bird) or you are likely to get **clattered** (hit) or she might **borst yer gob** (punch you in the mouth)
If you want to impress a lady buy her **'flooers'** (flowers)
If a lady or gentleman has a shapely bottom refer to it as a **'hintend'**
Geordie lads refer to their beloved lady as **'Wor Lass'**. Geordie Lasses refer to their beloved gentleman as **'Him'**

The Match

Saturdays are sacrosanct for a Propa and Posh Geordies. It is a day oot with their mates to watch the match and drink a lot of beor.
It can be summed up in five (four, really) words. Drink, Match, Drink, Curry, Home.

One of the greatest qualities of the Geordie is their eternal optimism and patience over the Toon football team. They have not won a major trophy for over 60 years. What really irritates a Geordie is a Manchester United, Manchester City or Liverpool fan whinging about not winning a trophy this season.

Watching the match - nothing gets in the way of a Geordie watching the Toon at St James Park or on the telly. Even their lass cannot get in the way! Even when the toon are away they will make a pilgrimage to the toon for a few beers and watch the match in a pub. I know many other teams fans do this, but it's in the Geordie genes to the point that even Gordon Banks (look him up – the best goalkeeper never to play for the toon!) couldn't stop him.

At a home match Geordies shout at every movement on the pitch but mostly at the referee. The crowd is often referred to as the 12th man but in the toon this is a certainty, all toon players experience this and never forget it.
A specialist trait of the Geordie football fan is bearing his chest in cold or inclement weather. Many supporters take off their shirt to show their incredible physique!! And of course, to show how hard they are!
Newcastle fans revel in the Makems defeats and misfortune – relegation.

This applies both ways, so the Makems love it when the Mags/Geordies lose or are relegated.

Bragging rights are very important to Geordies and Makems alike. Bragging is allowed in these circumstances. Makems and Geordies gain the bragging rights when their team have won the last match between them. Sunderland have those rights at the moment but Newcastle are in the Premier League and Sunderland are in the Championship. So, it's a good weekend if Sunderland lose.
If a Geordie ever feels sad, he remembers, that he could be a Makem. Now that is sad! (and vice versa!)

Other special dates for Geordie

There are two special dates for Geordies other than Home matches.
9 June – Blaydon Race Day and Great North Run weekend.
But any weekend is special to a Geordie. Oot in the toon is aalways special!!

Great north run ettyket

Run in a stupid costume to show how hard (physically) and soft-hearted Geordies are. Make sure you have many pints after the race to replenish the liquid you lost during it!

Entertaining at home – When Geordie has guests

Geordies expect guests in his home to bring food and drinks as a gift. Beer and crisps are acceptable.
When you are a guest, drink what you are given so long it is not wine. The standard response to being offered wine is 'Aa divvent drink fruit juice' Drink everything in the house even if there is only wine left! If you have not had enough get some from the off licence.
Never leave a party early. Stay till your host throws you out or when there's no more drink or crisps.
When drinking with friends or family at home it's rude to refill your glass only. Refill everyone's glass even if they don't want any – especially if they drink wine.

Hey there Geordie. It's bloody cold. You should put your coat on!
Hadaway and shite man. It's positively barmy

Shopping (therapy)

Geordie Lads hate shopping. They would rather be in the pub waiting for their lass to finish shopping.

Geordie Lads always walk 2 steps behind their lass - you never lead when your lass is shopping.

Geordie lasses always spend twice as long as they need to when looking at or for something in the shops.

When we say 'shopping' in the case of a Geordie Lass, we mean shopping for clothes, makeup, handbags and jewellry.

Geordie lads never wear matching clothes with their lass. Their mates will think your lass chose it, and it will cramp your style with other lass's.

When Geordie lasses wear a skirt or dress they make sure it FULLY covers their posterior. The question is not *'Does my bum look big in this?'* but *'Would Grandma be proud of this outfit?'*

Wear shorts as long as you can in the toon to show how hard you are. Scots copy Geordies by wearing a skirt! Scots wearing kilts are cissies. We all know they have their willy warmers on!

Geordies preferred dress is a Newcastle shirt and anything red and white is a big **No No.**

When shopping for clothes, say *claes.*
If buying footwear, refer to them as *byuts* (boots).

Essential words and phrases when in Geordieland

Geordies use certain words to disguise their conversation (cockneys copied this method in their quaint Cockney rhyming slang - Geordies invented words to disguise their drinking activities from their lass - a much more important reason than trying to confuse the police!! This is also a good reason why Geordies are excellent spy material!

Pronunciation

Castle not carstle
Garage not gararge
But plarster not plaster
Shite rather than Shit
Hoose rather than house
Bliddy not bloody
Warse not worse
Deed - not the act of doing something but dead
Numbers - One two three ok but fower, siven, Ayt.
Heed not to take note but head

General Rule
Use mind, like or man at the end of a sentence.

Aalreet bonny lad? - a polite way of saying hello.

Aalreet wor kid? - slang term for hello.

Aalreet mate, what ya uptee the morra? – Geordie phrase.
Hello, what are your plans for tomorrow? – Translation.

Aboot – about.
'How aboot gannin t' the toon the neet? ' 'How about going out in the Town tonight?'

Afeared – afraid.

'Aa'm afeared the toon are doomed this season.'

Amang – amongst.
'Hoe Geordie, let's get amang the lasses the neet!'

Backside – rear end, arse.
'Aa'll show me backside (arse) in Fenwick's window' – said when someone is very confident about something he or she has said and if they were wrong they would bare their posterior in the window of Newcastle's premier department store.
For example. 'Aa'd show me arse in Fenwick's window if Sunderland ever won the Premier League!'
This can be adapted to any department store or big shop in the area.

Bad or badly - ill or sick.
'Aa wus bad this morning after that session last neet in the toon, it must've been a bad pint'.
'After last night's drinking session I am not feeling very well. The amount I had to drink is irrelevant, only one must have upset my stomach'.

Bairns – children.
'Shy bairns get nowt' - shy children get nothing.
'He's like the bairns' – he is acting like a child.

Belta – excellent.
'The Toon played a belta on Saturday, like!'
'Newcastle United were excellent on Saturday.'

Big End – concert room in the club.
'Geordie, Aa'm gannin in the big end t' see the torn. Are yer comin'?'
'I am going in to the concert room to listen to the musical band. Are you coming with me George?'

Blather - to talk on and on and on.
'Y' knaa what Geordie, that Jeff Stelling dissent half blather on!'

'A right bobby dazzler' - someone who wears outrageously bright clothes, is very good looking or who thinks a lot of themselves.
"Look at that charva owa there; she thinks she's a reet bobby dazzla.

Bugger – a mild swear word often said as a term of amazement.
'Whey yer bugger, the Toon beat Manchester United the day!'

Bubble - to cry.
"The bairn's ganna bubble if there's nee pop left."
"My child is going to cry if there is no fizzy drink left."
If you feel emotional and want to express your emotion you are allowed to bubble. If Paul Gascoigne can do it, it's acceptable to all self-respecting Geordies.

Cack or Cacky – the brown stuff (Shite)
'Hoe Geordie when Aa saw that pollis aa nearly cacked mesell'
'Geordie, when I saw the policeman I nearly soiled myself'

Cannit - cannot
'Aa cannit see nee lasses'
'I cannot see any young ladies'

Canny - Good, friendly.
'He's a propa canny, lad.' 'He's a really nice person'
'He's geet canny as oot'' 'He is really friendly.'
'That film's (pronounced 'Filums') canny good, like'
'That film I watched last night was really good.'

Champion is the reply expressing that something is great, excellent or you are well.

Charva - Chav, a young person typified by brash and loutish behaviour and the wearing of (real or imitation) designer clothes.
'How man, have a deek at them charvas gannin' radgie owa there.'
'Hey! Have a look at those louts going crazy over there.'

Clag - to stick
'Aa'm ganna clag this poster t' the waal'
'I will paste this poster to this wall'

Clammin' – desperate or in some cases, hot
'Where's me fan am clammin''
'Where is my cooling fan I am glowing'
'Where's the chippy aam clammin'''
'Where is the fish and chip shop, i am very hungry'

Clammy – sweaty.
'Me hands are clammy'
'I am glowing'

Clappers – fast.
'Aa ran like the clappers t' catch that bus'
'I ran very fast to get the bus'

Clarts/Hacky - Clarts means mud or dirt and hacky means dirty.
'Divvent play in the clarts, y'll get hacky!'
'George don't play in the mud you will get dirty'
However, when someone is messing about or being very slow, they ***'Clart on'*** **or *'Fanny on'.***

Clivor – clever.
'He's a clivor sod'
'That man is too big for his britches'

Daft – not very bright.
'Are yee daft'
'Are you stupid'

Dee as yer telt! – 'Do as you're told!' – used to put naughty Geordies throwing ***radgies*** or being a proper ***workyticket***, back in their place.

Doon – down.
'Calm doon, aal mek a cuppa'
'Calm Down, I'll make a cup of tea'
'A'am gannin doon the toon!'
'I am travelling to the city centre'

Giz a deek – 'Let me have a quick peek (or look) at what you're doing'
"Giz a deek at ya cornet. You've got mare monkey's blood than me"
"Let me have a look at your ice cream. You've got more raspberry sauce than I have".

Dunch - to bump into someone or something.
'How, man, divvin' dunchus' – 'My friend, please do not bump into me'
'Aa'd luv t' dunce that car!' – I would like to bump that car that has just cut me up'.

'Dorsent' – dare not.
'Aa Dorsent dee that!
'I dare not do a bungee jump!' or 'I dare not tell my wife'

'Eee' – a word many Geordie lasses say before every sentence.
'Eee, Aa've chipped me nail varnish.'
'Well, I have damaged my nail varnish'.
'Eee, aa've laddad me tights.'
'Well, I have laddered my stockings'

Fetch - to bring.
'Hoe, Geordie fetch me shoes'
'George, would you please pass my shoes to me'

Fettle – a word with several meanings.
'In a fettle' - in a bit of a tizz or in a foul mood
'Out of Fettle' - not very well or feeling ill/out of sorts.
'To fettle someone' - to sort them out.
'Canny fettle' - you're feeling well and in good health.

Flee - not to run away but to fly.
'Aa'm fleeing oot t' Spain the neet'.
'I am flying out to Spain tonight'.

Fond - silly, foolish.
'Eee, he is fond'.
'Well, he is little foolish'

'Gadgie' - is an old man over the age of 40!
Made common by being heavily used in describing men over 40 running the Blaydon race. At 40 you are a G. At 70 a man would be classed as GGGGGG !

Gannies - little fingers.

Ganzee - raincoat

Giveowa – Give over.
If you want someone to stop doing something say 'Giveower'

Gyp – pain.
'Me knee's givin us gyp this mornin.'
'My knee is sore this morning, I fell down after a few pints'
Gob – mouth.
'Divvent shoot ya gob off, man.'
'Please don't shout, my friend.'

Had – Hold.
'Hoe mate, Had yer waata'
'My friend, could you just hold on a minute.'

'Haddaway' expression of negativity or disbelief.
"Haddaway, man, there's nee way Ronaldo is signing for the Toon."
"You're joking?! There is no way Ronaldo is signing for Newcastle United."
'Haddaway & shite' - Said in disbelief or for those in the know, a firm of solicitors in the toon.

Hackies – funny looks.
'Hoe man, he's givin' is hackies'
'He's giving me funny looks'.

Hellish – good, stylish, daring.
'Hoe Geordie, that ride at the Hoppings was hellish'
'George, that ride at the fair was very good'

Hinny or wor lass: Wife, female companion or life partner (could have been derived from Honey).
'Dee us some scran, hinny. I'm clamming.'
'Please, make me some food, my love. I'm very hungry.'

Hooly – strong wind.
'It's blaaain a hooly oot there!'
'It is very windy out there this morning'

Howk – to hit
'Your lass give ye a good howkin' last neet after that session'
'You wife clipped you across you ear last night. You were very drunk!'

Hoy - pass or throw. An alternative is used when out drinking as you 'hoy the drink doon yer neck.' Or 'On the Hoy'.
'Hoe Harry, Hoy the hamma owa here.' (only expert Geordies should attempt to say this phrase !!
'Harry, would you please pass the hammer over here.'
When Geordie is feeling sick after a session ' Howay Geordie, hoy it up son!'

Hunkas - crouching down low with your backside sitting on your calves and ankles.
'Get doon on ya hunkas man.'

'Howay man' - can be both positive and negative, for example, come on, get a grip or what are you doing?
'Howay the Toon'
'Come on Newcastle United you can do it!'
"Howay man! We gannin' doon the toon'
"Come on. We are going into the city centre"
'Howay man, doon yer pint wer' gannin t' the Toon Walls'
'You need to drink your pint, we are moving on to the next public house'
'Howay man, aa'm not 10 foot taal, that ball would ha' hit the top o' the Angel'
'What are you doing, you pass was far too high for me to reach'

Jarp - to strike or hit.
'Aa was jarpin' with the sprouters on Sunda'
'I was knocking boiled eggs together with the Children on Easter Sunday'

'Keks' – trousers.
"Geordie, Get your keks on.'

'Ket' – sweets or food with little value.
'How, man, divvin' nick aall me ket!'
'Please do not take all of my sweets'

Kite – belly.
'Hoe Geordie yer gettin' a bit of kite on there, son!'
'Geordie you are getting a big belly there, my friend.'

'Knaka' – Knacker – an uncouth, loutish person.
'That knaka Trump is a bit fond!'
No translation needed!

Lowp – to jump over
'Geordie, just lowp ower that fence man, we'll miss the bus!'
'Geordie, jump over the fence because we might miss the bus!'

Lug – ear.
'Aa'll clip yer lug if yer divvent shut up'
'I will strike your ear if you carry on speaking'

Lush – extremely good or nice.
'She's geet lush.'
'She's very good looking.'

Muggles - marbles not non-wizards.
'Let's play muggles, Geordie.'

Nebby – nosey.
'Divvent' be nebby' 'Don't be nosey'
'He's a reet nebby bugga'
'He is a very nosey person'

Netty – toilet.
'Where's ya netty, marra? I'm bustin''
'Where is the toilet please, my friend. I am desperate for the loo.'

Nithered – very cold.
'These southerners must be nithered, they've got their jumpers on'

Nowt – nothing.
'The toon were nowt nor summat the day!'
'Newcastle United did not play very well this afternoon.' Literally 'Newcastle United were nothing nor something this afternoon'

Paggered - exhausted or extremely tired.
'Aa'm paggered tryin' t' keep up wi' ye Geordie.' (Geordie's mate during a session on the hoy).

Pet – a word of affection not an animal.
'Aa luv yee pet'
'I love you, my darling wife'
'Cheers pet'
'Thank you very much, my darling.'

Ploatin' - raining
'It's ploatin' doon oot there'
'It's raining outside'

'Plodgin' – to wade in water.
'Aa wus plodgin' on Cullercoats beach the day. That North sea is nitherin' even for me'
'I was wading in the North Sea today at Cullercoats beach. It was very cold!'

Geordies at the seaside

All Geordies enjoy a plodge in the freezing North Sea.
All Geordies can brave the North Sea by fully immersing themselves because Geordies don't feel the caad (cold). See Geordie at a Toon Match!

Pollis – police.
"Divvent upset the Polis, Aa wanna finish me drink!.'

Posh Geordie – one who has a mild Geordie accent and tries to say certain words in the King's english.

Propa Geordie – one who has an unfettered Geordie accent

Pump - to break wind. Alternatively – fart.
'Geordie's been on the beer and he pumped (farted) in the chippy. He cleared the shop!' (no explanation needed!)

Radgie – losing one's temper
'That gadgie's gannin' proper radgie, like.'
'That gentleman is extremely cross.'
'Eee, he was gannin propa radge'
'Well, he was really angry'

Rift - to belch.
'Geordie, that curry is mekin' me rift like a pregnant coo.'
'That curry is making me belch very much.'

Sackless - useless or stupid, no sense'.
'Isn't that Trump Sackless' 'Nor, that's too good a word for him!'
(no explanation needed!)

Sartinly – certainly.
'Aaa sartinly wus well-oiled last neet at the club!'
'I was certainly very drunk last night.'

Scran – food.
'Where's me scran, I'm clamming.'
'I am looking forward to my meal. I am very hungry.'

Shooting and baalin' - Arguing with someone.
'There wus a lot o' shooting and baalin' last neet at the club.' A bloke got howked!'
'There was a large argument last night in the club. Someone was hit!'

The skitters – Dehli belly, diarrhoea.
''Aa had the skitters this morning, it must have been a bad pint!'
(no explanation needed!)

Snaa – snow.
'Aa think wh ganna get snaa the neet.'
'I think the weather forecaster says it will snow tonight.'

Sneck – latch or lock.
'Put the sneck on the netty door'
'Lock the door to the toilet, please.'

Spelk - Splinter of wood that gets stuck in a finger.
"Hoy is some tweezas owa here, hinny. I've got a spelk."
"Pass some tweezers, please darling. I have a splinter."

Sprouter - child
'The sprouters are comin' roond the neet t' watch the match'
'My children are coming to our house to watch the football on TV'

Stot - rebound or bounce.
'Aa'll stot your heed on that waal'
'If you say that again I will be very cross'

Stowed out - full to the gunnels or brim.
'Geordie, the neet club is stowed out wi' lasses and w' cannit get in! Bugger'
'Geordie the night club is full of delightful young ladies but we cannot get in, Damnation!'

Tappy Lappy – walking slowly.
'Aa wus tappy lappy doon the road and this lass looked at us and thouwt, she's a corker!'
'I was walking down the road and this young lady caught my eye and she was very nice'

Toon - Newcastle city centre or Newcastle United - all Geordie understand the context when using the word toon.

Varnigh – almost, very nearly.
'Aa wus varnigh full in the session last neet, Geordie.'
'I nearly had too many beers last night.'

Geet walla - Very, very large.
'Ha' yer seen the size o' her arse it's geet walla'
'Have you seen the size of the lady's posterior, it is rather large!'
Alternatively,
Ha' yer seen the size o' his Belly, it's geet walla!'

Wazzock - imbecile or fool. This is usually used as an insult!
'That gadgie's a propa wazzock.'
'That Trump is a fool'

Whey aye, man! – Well Yes, my friend. A proclamation of positivity or agreement.
'Whey aye, man! I'm oot on the toon the neet.'
'Yes, of course! I'm all for a night out in town.'

Whinge - to whine or complain incessantly.
'That Trumpis a bit of a whinger!'
No explanation needed!

'Worky (pronounced Warky) ticket' – someone who is being very annoying.
'Yor a proper workyticket, Ye!' When talking to a friend who is winding up his or her mates.
"The bairn's being a propa workyticket. If he's not careful there'll be nee ket this week."
"The little one is being very naughty. If he's not careful, there'll be no sweets this week."

Wor lass - my girlfriend, my wife or my partner.

Wor lad (or Him!) - my boyfriend, my husband, or my partner.

Wrang – wrong.
'Divvent get is wrang, pet'
'Don't get me wrong, my darling.'

Yark - to hit.

Yem - home
'Am knackered. Howay, pet, I'm gannin yem.'
'I'm very tired. Come on, darling, I'm going home."

Yit – yet.

Yous – the plural of you but said by many Geordies in that context.

Advanced Geordie!!

'Yee oot the neet, like?' '
'Aye, but am gannin canny. Aa woz oot wiv wor lass last neet.'
'Let us naa what ya deein if yee wanna gan for some scran or aal just gan yem.'

'Do you have plans tonight?' 'Yes, but not drinking too much, I was out with the wife last night.'
'Let me know what you are up to, if you want to go for something to eat or, if not, I will just go home.'

Giz a bag o'crisps - A Geordie put-down, usually declining a romantic advance.
'I'd rather not, thank you.'
'Howay man, divvin' be daft. Him? Giz a bag o' crisps.'
Come on, don't be stupid, I don't fancy him, he's not my type.'

'Harry Hoy the Hammer ower here'
'Harry would you please pass the hammer to me'

'He's a reet worky ticket him'

Geordie Haka

(https://www.youtube.com/watch?v=WpN5NyTSth8)

Howay
Anna ye
Anna ye
Anna ye naa
Anna ye naa me
Wor lad looks like this
Wor lad looks like that
Geet fat Knacka
Wor lad workin
Wor lad workin
Canny fiddle
Canny fiddle
Wees keys
Wees keys are these keys
Tattoo o me daa
Tattoo o me maa
Pint in this hand
Tab in this hand
Howay

Musical terms –
credit to Mark Deeks

Flat – NEE FIZZ!
Sharp – HOW THAT NACKED!
Pause – HAAD YA HORSES!
Semibreve Rest – EEE I'M KNACKERED!
Minim Rest – I'M GAN FOR A LIE DOON!
Crescendo – A CANNA HEAR YE PET!
Decrescendo – DIVVENT WAKE THE BAIRNS!
Repeat – A THINK A'L DEE THAT AGAIN!
FF (very loud) – GEET MASSIVE!
MF (moderately loud) – WEY IT COULD BE LOUDER!
PP (very soft) – THERE'S NOWT THERE!
MP (moderately soft) – CANNY SOFT!

Gentleman v Geordie Ettyket

Gentlemen	Geordie
Buy their clothes in Savile Row	There are nee claes shops in Savile row in the toon
Belong to a club	Every self-respecting Geordie belongs to their local working men's club or goes to a night club
Go fishing and sailing in the summer and shooting in colder seasons	Geordies divvent have time for fishin' and sailin', they are oot enjoyin' thesells aall the time
Hold doors open for people unnecessarily	Geordies always open doors for others
Say good morning to all the gentle folk although this may not to the lower classes	Geordies say hello to everyone. They have been in trouble before, terrifying Londoners by saying hello to them.
Say good morning to people they do not like	See above
Can be supercilious in their greeting habits and can greet each other like long lost lovers on first introduction	Geordies are never supercilious because they don't know what it means. See above.
Stand up and offer their seat to a lady	So do Geordies
Offer to carry what a lady is carrying even if she seems to be coping well with the load	So do Geordies
Offer ladies their arm	Geordies would rather cuddle them
Walk on the traffic side of the road	Geordies don't walk on the road it's too dangerous
Place a folded handkerchief in their breast pockets but never seem to blow their noses on them	What's a handkerchief?
Ask if anyone objects before lighting a cigarette	Geordies divvent smoke
Stand up if a lady leaves the room	If Geordies did, they would be up and doon like a yoyo!

Gentlemen do not Geordies do

Gentlemen	Geordie
Talk too loudly	Geordie do this all the time
Crack jokes	See above
Laugh uproariously	See above
Talk with your mouthful	See above
Butt in on someone else's anecdote	See above, it's part of the crack
Hog the conversation	Mates shout and baal so no one can hog the chat
Make personal comments	See answer to first line above
Answer your mobile phone while someone is talking to you	Only if it is their lass
Shuffle your feet constantly	See first line
Gesture wildly especially while holding a drink on the other hand	See above
Do not stand with your hands in your pockets	See above
Behave like a bore	One thing you can say about Geordies, they are never boring.
Talk exclusively about yourself	Geordies never do this, it's all about football!

How to tell if you've drunk too much

Gentlemen	Geordie
You drop your posh accent	Geordies divvent have one in the forst place.
You laugh too loudly and too long	Geordies dee this aal the time
You become lewd and lascivious	Geordies divvent knaa what that means
You shout at the waiter as if he were deaf	Geordies dee that when sober
You ask the waitress to dinner	All members of the female gender are fair game
You forget you are engaged to be married	Geordies would never do that, their life wouldn't be worth living if their lass fund oot.
You eat a kebab	Life wouldn't be worth living without a kebab after a session
You begin to sing football anthems	What!!!! Saturdays wouldn't be the same at the match

Geordie-ness Test

So, being a welcoming bunch, the level of Geordie status could be something that non-Geordies can achieve.
There are many great examples of adopted Geordies that Tynesiders have taken to their hearts: some are born Geordie, some achieve Geordie-ness and some have Geordie-ness thrust upon them.
But how Geordie are you?
The Chronicle compiled 100 of rites-of-passage events for a 'How Geordie Are You?' challenge. 100 questions, one point for each positive reposnse.

Have ridden the front seat of the Metro?
Been to the hoppings?
Eaten a Ham and pease pudding stottie?
Paddled at Longsands, Tynemouth?
Been to St James Park?
Been to see Fenwicks window at Christmas?
Walked along the Gateshead Millennium bridge?
Done the Angel at the Angel of the North?
Been to Beamish Museum?
Been to Plate day, Newcastle Races?
Eaten a Greggs pastie?
Gone to a panto at the Theatre Royal?
Been drinking in the Bigg market?
Been drinking on the Quayside?
Been drinking on Osborne road?
Been drinking on the Diamond strip?
Can sing all the verses of the Blaydon races?
Can quote lines from Auf Wiedersehen Pet?
Been out on a Friday night in January with no coat?
Had a walk in Jesmond Dene?
Bought a copy of Viz?
Gone up the lifts in the Baltic?
Gone to an exhibition in the Baltic?
Gone to an exhibition in the Laing Art Gallery?
Get a regular delivery from Ringtons?
Bought something from the Quayside Sunday Market?
Drunk a bottle of Newcastle Brown Ale?
Stood in a cow pat on the Town Moor?

Have used the phrase 'Howay the lads'?
Seen a film at the Tyneside Cinema?
Met someone at the Greys monument?
Admired the view from the Free Trade Inn?
Eaten a knickerbocker glory at Mark Toney?
Got emotional at seeing the Tyne Bridge?
Gone to a concert at the City Hall?
Have been on stage at the City Hall?
Gone to the Great North Museum?
Gone to Seven Stories?
Gone to a concert at the Sage
Watched the Great North Run?
Have run the Great North Run?
Have watched the Falcons rugby team?
Have watched the Eagles basketball team?
Visited more than one Roman Wall site?
Own a Lindisfarne album?
Have given directions to a stag or hen party?
Described something as 'canny'?
Described something a 'hacky'?
Sledged down Cow Hill?
Have done a Boxing Day dip?
Eaten a curry after midnight?
Had a letter published in the Journal or the Chronicle?
Have been in a story in the Journal or the Chronicle?
Have seen the Swing Bridge swing?
Have eaten Pan Haggerty?
Have rung night owls?
Have run the Blaydon race?
Have used the Shields ferry?
Have seen athletics at the Gateshead Stadium?
Have walked through the Tyne Pedestrian tunnel?
Have seen Vera being filmed?
Have described someone as 'radgie'?
Have gone up Greys monument?
Have seen Ant and Dec (not on the telly) ?
Have seen Cheryl (not on the telly or in concert) ?
Have seen Alan Shearer (not on the telly or playing football) ?
Have seen a red squirrel?

Have had a canny bag of Tudor crisps?
Have gone to Tynemouth Sunday market?
Have never watched Geordie Shore?
Called splinters 'spelks'?
Call tell the difference between Geordie and makem accents?
Had fish and chips at Colmans?
Have travelled the Metro coastal loop all the way round?
Have gone to the Metro Centre for a night out?
Have bought fruit from the Grainger Market?
Have had Chinese food at Stowell street?
Have gone ice skating at the Centre for Life?
Have walked through the Victoria tunnel?
Know someone who grew up with Sting?
Have gone to the Discovery museum?
Have climbed to the very top of the Castle Keep?
Have given money to a busker in the Central Arcade?
Are a member of the Literary and Philosophical society?
Have seen a play at the Northern Stage?
Have seen inside the Mansion House?
Have been to a service at St Nicholas's Cathedral or St Mary's Cathedral?
Have bought something at the Barbour factory shop?
Have gone to the dogs or speedway at Brough Park?
Have seen the City Centre model in the Civic Centre?
Have been to a concert by the Royal Northern Sinfonia?
Have eaten a Greggs pastie on coming home to Newcastle Airport
Have run up the sides of the underpass to Exhibition Park?
Have thrown a shoe at the shoe tree in Armstrong park?
Know someone who was in Byker Grove?
Have seen the heads move behind Rosie's bar?
Have met one of the Animals?
Have run all the way up the escalator at Haymarket metro station?
Knows someone who went to school with Jimmy Nail?
Have won a leek show?

Unless you've got at least 50% we reckon you've got some way to go - but at least this gives you a bucket list for Geordie self-improvement.
Anything above 75% is pretty good and if you've get into the 90s, you're probably Jimmy Nail! Me, I got 72!